*Cotswold Scene*

First published in Great Britain in 1996 by
Chris Andrews Publications
15 Curtis Yard North Hinksey Lane
Oxford OX2 0LX  Tel: 01865-723404
Revised and Updated 1999,2006
Photographed and produced by Chris Andrews,
with additional images from Angus Palmer
Westonbirt pictures by Derek Harris
Photographs of Blenheim Palace by kind permission
of His Grace The Duke of Marlborough.
Photograph on p67 by kind permission of
The Benedictine Community of Prinknash

Photographs from The Oxford Picture Library.
Text by Fiona Danks
Design by Mike Brain
Edited by David Huelin
All material © Chris Andrews
ISBN: 1-905385-10-2
ISBN13: 978-1-905385-10-2
Colour reproduction, printing and binding in Great Britain
by Butler and Tanner Ltd, Frome and London

Front cover — *Naunton*
Back cover — *The Cotswolds at Cleeve Hill near Cheltenham*
Title page — *Winson*

# Cotswold Scene

*Photographed by Chris Andrews*
*Text by Fiona Danks*

# CONTENTS

# THE COTSWOLDS

For some people the name 'Cotswolds' conjures up a picture of sheltered valleys harbouring villages of honey-coloured stone beside clear, fast-flowing streams. Others may think of high, bleak, open countryside criss-crossed by dry-stone walls, or bustling old market towns with their perpendicular churches. However it is pictured, this area close to the heart of England has long been a popular destination for visitors, its mellow buildings being an integral part of the landscape rather than an infliction upon it.

The Cotswolds are often described mistakenly as hills, but they form part of a limestone mass tilting gently down to the south-east and split by many river valleys. The name 'Cotswold' was originally given to the area of the River Windrush, with its headwaters up on the high 'wolds', a word used to describe a bare hill or upland common. 'Cod' was a Saxon leader who farmed around the source of the Windrush about 1200 years ago; some say that this is the derivation of 'Cot', while others prefer the old English word for 'sheep enclosure'. This too is a plausible explanation because, along with stone, sheep have been the key to the creation of the Cotswolds we see today.

The area that we now call the Cotswolds is defined both by the underlying stone and by its use as a building material. It is the highest part of a band of oolitic limestone that extends from the Dorset coast north-eastwards to Lincolnshire. Laid down millions of years ago beneath a warm shallow sea, oolite, or roe-stone, has an egg-like structure resembling fish roe. This grainy rock not only provides the landscape's shape and form but has for thousands of years provided an excellent building material, soft enough to be sawn but hardening into a durable stone on exposure to the air. The stone is so easy to work and is in such plentiful supply that it has been used in all types of buildings, from stone walls and humble cottages to churches, manor houses and palaces. The earliest evidence of the craft of the stonemason is at Belas Knap long barrow near Winchcombe, built by Stone Age people 4000 years ago. One of the finest long barrows in the country, it consists of a stone-roofed chamber covered by grass and flanked by dry-stone walls. These walls are built with great skill, and are closely resembled by the walls that are such a notable feature of today's Cotswolds.

Situated high on a hillside, Belas Knap was built when the valleys were densely wooded and difficult to defend. About that time hunter-gatherers were beginning to clear land for farming, preferring to clear woodland from the lighter soils on the hills rather than from the heavier valley soils. The Iron Age tribes organized themselves into bigger groups and began to build large earthen forts in strategic positions, particularly along the western Cotswold edge.

The high wold land, already important for farming, was easily defended from marauders by forts such as the one at Little Sodbury.

The next people to leave their mark on the Cotswolds were the Romans, who established a military zone here, subduing the native Dobunni tribesmen. Some of the busiest modern highways follow the routes of military roads built by legionaries between AD43 and 49; the Fosse Way, Ermin Street and Akeman Street all meet at Cirencester. Built of readily available local stone, these routes serviced the prosperous civilization that existed here for about 400 years. The Roman rulers lived very comfortably, as can be seen from the ruins of the villa at Chedworth near Northleach and the remains in Bath and Cirencester. They established towns and farmed the land, bringing the long-wool sheep from the Mediterranean to improve native flocks and to provide warm clothes for troops unaccustomed to cold weather. There is some evidence to suggest that the Dobunni were encouraged to export woollen cloaks to Rome.

The Roman legions were recalled in AD406 and the land was re-conquered by Angles and Saxons. They reached the Cotswolds about AD600, and Gloucester and Winchcombe became important centres standing on the volatile Wessex-Mercia border. Many timber villages were built both on the plateau and along spring lines, leaving us a legacy of place names with Anglo-Saxon origins. The name is often all that remains, for the Saxons used little stone until after the seventh century when Christianity spread and the pious began to build small stone churches.

Most of the land was in the hands of the abbeys, who continued to clear woodland and scrub to create extensive sheep-walks; the climate, landscape and downland lent themselves well to sheep rearing. The hardy Cotswold sheep, descended from the 'Long-wool' was gaining a reputation for its large, high quality, hard-wearing and lustrous fleece and was probably the main breed used in the area. As early as the eighth century wool was being exported to Flemish and Italian weavers. By the time of the Domesday survey in 1086 most of the present-day villages existed and there was an open field system for sheep-grazing and arable farming. The only substantial woodlands were found along the escarpment edge and in the royal forests at Cirencester and Wychwood. There were very few larger settlements and the only market town was Winchcombe.

Following the Norman conquest in 1066, central power moved to London and the south-east but many churches and abbeys were built in the Cotswolds. The Normans had a strong tradition of building in stone, and the Cotswold stone had qualities similar to their own oolites around Caen. The monasteries grew wealthy and were often more concerned about their valuable sheep flocks than about the welfare of people, sometimes demolishing whole villages to create more grazing land. Wool exports became a mainstay of the economy during the twelfth century when weavers in Flanders needed increasing quantities to supply a growing population. By 1275 Edward I was charging a levy on all wool exports. Regular wool fleets were sailing across the channel by the fifteenth century, when the country had become so dependent upon wool that the Lord Chancellor's seat in the House of Lords came to be called the 'Woolsack', a name that remains to this day. The Cotswold area thrived upon the wool trade; wool producers, wool merchants and middlemen known as wool staplers all became wealthy.

Many of the small market towns were first established by the Normans. The Lord of the Manor or the monastery would buy a charter from the king giving permission to hold a weekly market. This then encouraged local trade and provided a regular income for the landowner. From the fourteenth century most of these towns became dependent upon the wool industry for their wealth. Places such as Chipping Campden, Northleach, Cirencester and Winchcombe became bustling communities where rich merchants built substantial houses and fine perpendicular churches. Many great stone barns were built; initially some were tithe barns where wool and corn levied by the monks were collected, but later they were used for storing fleeces and keeping them secure from thieves. The buoyant

*Cotswold Scene*

economy, plentiful stone and skilled masons ensured that there was a building boom. After the Dissolution of the Monasteries in 1539 there was a transfer of power and land into private hands. Many of the stonemasons previously employed by the monasteries became available for building houses for those who had benefited financially from the Dissolution.

Alongside the export business an active wool-processing industry began to develop. Initially this was a cottage industry, with the wealthy merchants buying and distributing the wool to poorly paid spinners and weavers working at home. Edward III encouraged weavers, dyers and fullers from Flanders to settle in England to stimulate production of woollen cloth. Fulling mills were built in the Cotswolds from as early as the twelfth century, powered by the clear fast-flowing streams. The fulling process originally involved treading or beating the cloth in running water to make the fibres 'felt' together, producing a more weather-resistant cloth. It was then found that the process was improved if the fabric was first scoured with 'fuller's earth' clay deposits of which are found in the valleys along the western escarpment. By the end of the sixteenth century the cloth industry was concentrated round Stroud.

The parliamentary enclosures between 1700 and 1840 caused great changes to the landscape. Over 120,000 acres of open sheep-walk and arable land were enclosed by walls and hedges; coverts and shelter belts were planted for shooting and vast areas of grassland were ploughed. While land was being enclosed, wool production was increasing in other parts of the world and the heavily taxed Cotswold wool could no longer compete. The 'Golden Age' of the Cotswolds was over and the region suffered the consequences of having relied so heavily upon one trade. Farm workers, weavers, spinners and others were reduced to a subsistence living and many buildings fell into decay. It is ironic that the rich legacy of fifteenth and sixteenth-century buildings that visitors come to see today is partly the result of this period of poverty, when there were no funds available for new building work. The more urban and industrial western valleys went into

*Bath*

decline during the nineteenth century, when the bulk of cloth manufacture moved to Yorkshire.

The nineteenth century brought mixed fortunes to the Cotswolds; while some areas were gentrified by the wealthy, others became depressed and neglected. With the development of better quarrying equipment, larger quantities of stone became available and many substantial country houses were built. Some market towns and villages suffered from extreme poverty while their wealthy neighbours visited each other's estates and enjoyed the prosperous spas of nearby Cheltenham and Bath.

Towards the end of the nineteenth century the area was 'discovered' by several well-meaning philanthropists, who appreciated it for its remarkable architectural wealth and unity. One of the first people to recognise the value of Cotswold buildings and countryside was William Morris, who had a country house at Kelmscott near Lechlade from 1871. Despite his unrealistic vision of a rural utopia full of contented craftsmen, he had a considerable influence upon the Cotswolds. In 1879 he founded the Society for the Protection of Ancient Buildings. It was his belief in the value of traditional building skills that inspired a group of architects and craftsmen to set up the Arts and Crafts movement, seeking to revive old English traditions and vernacular architecture. He once said 'These old buildings do not belong to us only . . . They are not in any sense our property, to do as we like with. We are only trustees for those who come after us'. All subsequent societies concerned with building conservation have remembered Morris's words. The beginning of the Cotswold tourist industry was possibly the publication of a book by an Oxford don, Herbert Evans. Following a cycling tour in 1905 he wrote the first descriptive history of the area; like Morris he was impressed by the architecture but appalled by the sorry state of repair of many churches.

Although Cotswold stone buildings are found outside the region, other materials are rarely used within it. Stone can be found very near the surface; on some hills the soil is only about 15cm thick, and oolite chunks can be seen

*Bibury, Arlington Row.*

in newly ploughed fields. At one time there were hundreds of small quarries, most of them on common land. It was small-scale quarrying that created the built environment of most of the Cotswolds; whole villages would be built of stone from a local quarry, resulting in harmony of colour. There have also been several larger quarries, as at Leckhampton, which supplied stone for Regency Cheltenham.

There are considerable variations in the colour and quality of the stone; nearest to the surface it is known as 'ragstone' and is often broken into uneven wedges, suitable for dry-stone walls or plain farm buildings. Beneath this layer is found the Great Oolite and then the Inferior Oolite, inferior implying 'beneath' rather than 'poor quality'. Easily hewn and shaped, both oolites are known as 'freestone' and make excellent building material. They can be cut into smooth-surfaced blocks called 'ashlar', or sculpted into window surrounds and mouldings. There is quite a range of colours; the inferior oolites tend to have a higher iron content and thus a richer yellow colour. In the north the stone is a deep golden colour, near Painswick it is silver-grey and in the south it is honey-gold. Cotswold stone has been much praised for its apparent ability to retain light; J.B. Priestley said that it 'knew the trick of keeping the lost sunlight of centuries glimmering'.

A unique feature of Cotswold buildings is the use of stone roofing slates, although many of the humbler cottages were originally thatched. In some places the lower beds of Great Oolite split into layers to form natural slates, referred to by masons as 'presents'. The source of many slates was Stonesfield near Woodstock. The area round the village is pitted with old quarries from which stone was removed to be laid in the fields and exposed to the frost which caused it to split. The slates would then be cut and shaped by skilled masons. The use of stone slates declined when Welsh slates became more readily available in the nineteenth century, brought here on the new railways.

The traditional Cotswold building style arose out of need rather than a desire to please. Originating in the fifteenth century, the deceptively simple style was defined by the limits of stone technology, which naturally produced buildings of similar characters. The notable features include steeply pitched stone slate roofs with gabled dormer windows, stone gables, centrally placed mullioned windows, rectangular dripstones and tall stone chimneys. The uneven slates readily absorbed water, so a steep pitch was necessary to repel as much rainfall as possible. Rectangular dripstones ensured the water would not run down the absorbent walls. Most of the early cottages would have been single storey with steep straw thatch roofs. Straw was widely available and cheap, so the slate was reserved for the better buildings. By the seventeenth century slate was more widely used and often replaced thatch on cottages when a second floor with dormer windows was added. There are many variations on the basic building style, the larger and more affluent buildings having more elaborate carving.

It is not only the buildings but also the dry-stone walls that are an integral part of the Cotswold landscape. Many walls originate from the peak of the enclosure period in the mid-eighteenth century, and they follow, and therefore seem to stress, the undulations of the hills. Often built of stone dug on site, they were carefully placed in courses, the stones being laid in the same way as they had been found. The wall was topped by a layer of vertical stones known as 'combers'. The stone walls, built with great skill, provided excellent stockproof barriers but the oolite weathers and shatters easily, so without regular maintenance the walls deteriorate.

Visitors are drawn to the Cotswolds for the landscape as well as the buildings. Like most landscapes in Britain, it is far from 'natural' and has been managed ever since Iron Age people first began to clear the original oak, elm, lime and hazel forest. At the height of the wool industry it was a wild, bleak place, with vast open sheep-walks. The greatest change probably took place when the open field system was abolished, with new walls, hedges and trees breaking up the rather featureless scene. The Cotswold landscape is full of contrasts, from the openness of the wolds

*Summer flowers at Chipping Campden.*

to the cosy verdant valleys, so well described by Laurie Lee; 'Living down there was like living in a bean-pod; one could see nothing but the bed one lay in. Our horizon of woods was the limit of our world'.

*Cider with Rosie* describes a rural way of life that disappeared forever with the increasing technological changes of this century, as 'time squared itself, and the village shrank, and distances crept nearer'. The development of the motor car made the Cotswolds accessible to increasing numbers of people, bringing more tourists and new residents. With more demand for housing, cottages were restored, not always appropriately, and new houses were built of a cheap mix of cement and crushed stone. Agriculture changed dramatically too, with much permanent pasture being ploughed for the first time to make way for cereals. There has been a further decline in sheep rearing and a move towards beef and dairy farming, with flower-rich limestone meadows being replaced by higher-yielding monocultures of rye grass. Many stone walls are collapsing and harsh new farm buildings have been built. Although the total area of woodland has remained almost unchanged, its quality has altered radically, with a loss of ancient deciduous trees in favour of faster-growing conifers.

During the 1960s there was increasing concern about the changes to the Cotswold landscape. In 1966 some 800 square miles were designated as an Area of Outstanding Natural Beauty (AONB). In 1990 this was extended to include parts of West Oxfordshire and an area around Bath. The Cotswolds is the largest of 41 AONB's in England and Wales, now covering 790 square miles. This recognizes the quality of the landscape, and there is a need to strike a balance between conservation and modern living. Tourists bring jobs and revenue, but must not spoil what they come to see. Incomers restore crumbling buildings but bring with them their suburban attitudes. New buildings should be constructed of traditional building materials and yet no one likes unsightly quarries marring the landscape.

Despite the potential for conflict, much is being done to retain the region's identity without fossilizing it. Strict controls over insensitive building developments ensure that unspoilt villages are conserved. Good quality and recycled stone are used for restoring old buildings or for new houses in sensitive locations, and reconstructed stone is used in other places. Regulations on the modernization of cottages and conversion of barns try to ensure that the external appearance is altered as little as possible.

The rural landscape is enjoyed by many visitors, for picnics, walks along the many footpaths and the 100-mile Cotswold Way, and for the region's rich natural history. Open spaces and nature reserves are managed by a variety of organizations, the AONB is looked after by the Cotswold Conservation Board a statutory body comprising a small team of staff, 40 Board members and Cotswold volunteer Wardens. The Boards duties are to conserve and enhance the natural beauty of the AONB and to increase the understanding and enjoyment of its special qualities. Some villages have remained as quiet backwaters, whereas others have been developed as honey-pots for visitors. Tourism is vital to the local economy; twelve per cent of the workforce rely upon it – twice the national average.

The character of many Cotswold towns and villages has been successfully preserved while allowing them to function in the modern world. Following its depression in the eighteenth and nineteenth centuries, the Cotswolds has been given a new lease of life. The Cotswold sheep has experienced a similar fate; once prized for its wool, it went into decline and was almost forgotten. There is now a renewed interest in old breeds and numbers of this large, hardy, long-wool animal are increasing as more people come to realize why it was so valuable in the first place.

*Fields east of Bibury at dawn.*

*Crickley Hill.*

*The Windrush Valley with Leafield church on the horizon.*

# STRATFORD AND CHIPPING CAMPDEN TO STOW

The northern area of the Cotswolds contains three well-known and contrasting towns; Moreton-in-Marsh is the principal town of the area, Chipping Campden a famous wool town and Stow-on-the-Wold 'where the wind blows cold'. There are extensive areas of true 'high wold', where arable farming dominates in an open and bleak landscape that was once grass- covered sheep-walk.

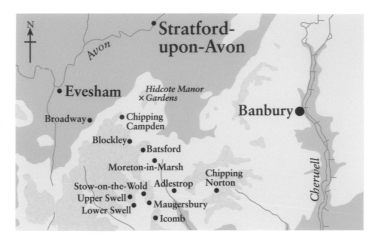

Many visitors to the Cotswolds approach from the north, using Stratford-upon-Avon as a base from which to explore. There is no true 'gateway' to the Cotswolds from this direction, but the natural amphitheatre of Dover's Hill near Chipping Campden offers views of all the Cotswold elements. From here the visitor can see the undulating landscape crossed with dry-stone walls; old stone houses and a 'wool' church blend perfectly into the scene as if they had always been there. Looking down the escarpment there are views over the Vale of Evesham towards the Malvern Hills.

Dover's Hill was threatened by developers in 1926 but was purchased by benefactors and given to the National Trust to conserve as public open space. On the Friday evening of Spring Bank Holiday thousands of people flock here for the Dover's Hill Games, a modern revival of the 'Cotswold Olympicks'. This annual sporting event was first held in or about 1612, founded by a local lawyer, Robert Dover. James I gave the games his royal approval, and they were possibly visited by Shakespeare. The games attracted people from all walks of life and included events such as shin-kicking, horse racing, coursing, running and wrestling; today's games have a rather more mild-mannered range of sports. It was always a lively and boisterous event but in the mid-nineteenth century there were riots in nearby Chipping Campden and the games were banned. It was not until the Festival of Britain in 1951 that they were revived, albeit in a slightly different form. The original games were very well known and are mentioned in social and  literary histories of Britain and in documents of the Olympic movement.

# CHIPPING CAMPDEN

Campden was granted a borough market in 1173 and was carefully planned by Hugh de Gondeville, the Lord of the Manor. The High Street was lined with small shops on long narrow burgage plots running back to service lanes. This layout remains but early wooden structures were replaced by stone buildings from as early as the fourteenth century.

Campden prospered with the wool trade, and was home to the best-known Cotswold wool merchant William Grevel, whose wealth was such that he lent money to Richard II. St. James's church is adorned with his memorial brass, the largest in Gloucestershire, which describes him as the 'flower of all wool merchants of England'.

With the decline of the wool industry came poverty; a quarter of the population left. In 1902 C.R.Ashbee set up the 'Guild of Handicrafts' with London craftsmen. Although the Guild lasted only six years, it re-vitalized the town and some craftsmen remained; the grandson of one of the original guild is a silversmith here. Ashbee restored Grevel's house and laid the foundations of the 'Campden Trust', which has helped to preserve many buildings.

*The town from the Cotswold Way to the north.*

*The Market Hall, built 1627 by local benefactor Sir Baptist Hicks to provide cover for produce stalls.*

*The torchlight procession and marching band at the conclusion of the Dover's Hill Games.*

*The town from the south, with St. James, the fifteenth-century 'wool' church.*

*Shakespeare's birthplace.*

Situated north of the Limestone belt and beside the River Avon, Stratford with its half-timbered buildings does not pretend to be a Cotswold town but it is a gateway to the northern Cotswolds.

Stratford ('street across the ford') was a river crossing in Roman times. Two Anglo-Saxon settlements later joined to become a market in 1196. It thrived as a busy market town, and at the time Shakespeare was a child his father the mayor welcomed groups of actors to entertain the townspeople. This may have started Shakespeare's interest in the theatre, which led him to London to work, but he returned to Stratford near the end of his life.

Although Stratford is barely twenty miles from the Cotswolds, Shakespeare wrote little about the area although he may have visited relations near Dursley. In Richard the Second, Act II, Scene iii, he describes the wilds of Gloucestershire thus:

'I am a stranger here in Glostershire:
These high wild hills and rough uneven ways
Draw out our miles and make them wearisome.'

*The house at Wilmcote where Shakespeare's mother, Mary Arden, lived.*

*Anne Hathaway's Cottage at Shottery.*

*Holy Trinity Church and the River Avon.*

# BLOCKLEY

Apart from its golden stone, Blockley bears some resemblance to the villages of the Stroud valley, with mills set amidst rows of cottages clinging to steep valley sides. During the eighteenth century when the wool industry was in decline, Blockley turned to silk production. By 1884 six silk mills powered by the fast-flowing Blockley brook provided work for about 600 people, preparing silk for ribbon-making factories in Coventry. This small centre of industry began to decline after 1860 when the levy on imported silk was removed.

Georgian cottage terraces built along the High Street during the early nineteenth century lack the typically 'Cotswold style' seen in older buildings dating back to the height of the wool trade. They do, however, have their own charm and significance in the history of the region.

Near the brook is a house called 'Fish Cottage', inlaid with a memorial tablet to a fish that died in 1855. Mr William Keyte had trained the fish to rise to the surface and feed out of his hand, and wished his friend to be remembered.

*Georgian terrace house.*

# BATSFORD

Batsford House and the arboretum were created in the nineteenth century by Lord Redesdale, alias Bertie Mitford, grandfather of the Mitford girls. After inheriting the estate from his uncle he demolished the existing house, replacing it with a golden ashlar mansion in the Cotswold Elizabethan style. At an entrance to the grounds the Victorian cottages of the estate village echo the local style, and the church of St. Mary's, built in 1862, is Neo-Norman.

Situated on a south-east facing slope overlooking Moreton-in-Marsh and the Evenlode, Batsford's soils vary from free-draining limestone soils on the higher slopes to heavy clay in the valley, thus suiting a wide variety of plants. Statues of Buddha, a Chinese temple and many oriental plants reflect Bertie Mitford's interest in China and Japan.

Mitford's son sold the estate to Sir Gilbert Wills, who became the first Lord Dulverton. The garden had been neglected but was later restored and expanded by the second Lord Dulverton, who died in 1992. Visitors can now enjoy one of the finest collections of trees in the country.

Batsford

# MORETON-IN-MARSH

Moreton is the principal town of the northern Cotswolds, situated on the Fosse Way and is served by the Cotswold Line railway. It grew up in the thirteenth century as a market town, with a wide main street, narrow burgage plots and back lanes. There is still a busy Tuesday market, with about 200 stalls attracting many visitors. On the first Saturday of September the town hosts one of the biggest one-day agricultural and horse shows in Britain.

Although Moreton was involved in the wool industry it does not have many buildings resulting from earlier prosperity. The oldest building is probably the sixteenth-century Curfew tower on the High Street; its bell was rung nightly until 1860 to remind people of the risk of fire at night.

Moreton has been a travellers' town for at least 1,700 years. It was used as a coaching station before the coming of the Oxford to Worcester railway in 1853. The High Street has many elegant eighteenth-century inns and houses, including the Redesdale Market Hall, a Victorian 'Tudor' building of some distinction. The Parish church, St. David's, was originally a chapel of ease for Bourton-on-the-Hill; in 1858 it was rebuilt in medieval style.

*The town from the north-west.*

*Moreton Show.*

*Moreton Show.*

# ADLESTROP

*The Old Rectory.*

Three miles east of Stow the village of Adlestrop stands near the Oxford to Worcester railway line. This is one of only three railways still open in the Cotswolds; the others are in the South-west passing through Stroud and a short stretch of line near Winchcombe, now operating steam trains.

Yes, I remember Adlestrop –
The name, because one afternoon
Of heat the express-train drew up there.
Unwontedly. It was late June.

Thus wrote the poet Edward Thomas before the First World War, making Adlestrop a familiar name among his readers. The large chocolate and cream Great Western sign that inspired Thomas was moved to the bus shelter when the railway station was closed. Amongst the village's stone cottages is the thatched old post office, and an elegant seventeenth-century former rectory in a quiet corner beside the church of St. Mary. Theophilus Leigh, Rector 1717–1763 and master of Balliol, lived in the rectory for many years. He was succeeded by his nephew and son-in-law, Thomas Leigh, whose niece and occasional visitor was Jane Austen.

*The Post Office.*

# STOW-ON-THE-WOLD

*The market square.*

At 229 metres Stow is the highest Cotswold town, and a hub from which seven roads radiate. The original settlement was at Maugersbury, but the importance of Stow as a road junction made it ideal for a market, and from 1107 it was renowned for its two annual Charter fairs. Daniel Defoe recorded seeing 20,000 sheep sold here in the early eighteenth century. With the decline in sheep farming the fairs turned to the horse trade, but nowadays they are mainly funfairs.

In 1646 the Battle of Stow raged nearby; this last important encounter of the Civil War led to nearly 1000 Royalist troops being imprisoned here by Cromwell. Even the church of St.Edward was used to confine prisoners. By 1657 the church was ruinous; it was restored in the 1680s, in 1847, and again in 1873, retaining few of its original characteristics.

For hundreds of years water was available only from springs below the town. It was carried up the hill until 1871 when Lord of the Manor Joseph Chamberlayne funded the construction of a deep well. In 1878 the grateful townspeople renovated the market cross to record their thanks.

*Stow from Adlestrop.*

*Aerial view of the town centre.*

*Feeding sheep at Maugersbury.*

# BROADWAY TO CHELTENHAM AND GLOUCESTER

This north-western area contains examples of all the distinctive landscapes that make up the Cotswolds, from the steep western escarpment to the high open wold and the wooded valleys with their fast-flowing streams. Just below the escarpment lie the cathedral city of Gloucester and the Regency Spa town of Cheltenham. North of Cheltenham and protruding beyond the general line of the escarpment are Oxenton Hill and Bredon Hill, remnants of the former scarp face that lay farther west.

Overlooking Cheltenham from the north-east is Cleeve Hill, the last unenclosed area of high wold and at 330 metres the highest point of the AONB, offering spectacular views over the Severn Valley. This area of common land is a Site of Special Scientific Interest (SSSI), its unimproved grassland supporting a wealth of wild flowers and butterflies. Cattle and sheep roam freely, grazing the area and maintaining it as open pasture. Such grasslands once dominated the Cotswolds but are now restricted to areas of common land or hillsides too steep to plough.

Along the escarpment, south-west of Cleeve Hill, lies Leckhampton Hill with its famous pinnacle of rock known as the Devil's Chimney. This strange column of rock was left by quarrymen but local legend has it that the stone rises straight from Hell. It first became a familiar landmark when the Great Western Railway pictured it on posters advertising the area; flocks of visitors caused serious erosion but a costly repair job ensured its survival as a Cotswold attraction. Now an SSSI for its natural grasslands, Leckhampton Common is pock-marked with old quarries. Stone for the building of Regency Cheltenham came from here and the old quarry face clearly reveals the layers of oolitic limestone. This and other old quarries along this western edge provide happy hunting grounds for fossil enthusiasts.

Gloucester cathedral's tall tower is clearly visible from many points along the scarp edge. Built of silver-grey Painswick stone, the cathedral dominates this city which has been capital of its shire since Saxon times. Its strategic location on the Severn was carefully chosen, giving good access to the south-west, Wales and the Cotswolds.

# BROADWAY

Sometimes described as the 'Show village of England', Broadway has been popular with visitors since it was 'discovered' by William Morris in the nineteenth century. He stayed frequently at Broadway Tower, from where he wrote the letter that led to the formation of the Society for the Protection of Ancient Buildings. The 'broad way' leads from the foot of the western escarpment; this wide grass-fringed street is lined with a pleasing variety of yellow stone buildings.

Broadway became a busy staging post on the route from Worcester to London as coaches had to harness extra horses for the long pull up Fish Hill. Many inns were opened, most notably the Lygon Arms that was bought from General Lygon by his butler in a shrewd business investment. The coming of the railway brought a period of quiet until the village was popularized by Victorian writers and artists; J.M.Barrie, Vaughan Williams and Elgar were among those who drew inspiration from the harmony of the Cotswold architecture. Nowadays Broadway caters for hordes of visitors with its shops, inns and cafes but still retains much of its charm.

*The Church of St. Michael and All Angels on the western edge of the village.*

*The village at dusk.*

*Broadway Tower, built 1799 by the Earl of Coventry as a present for his wife.*

*Like Buckland, Laverton lies on the spring line beneath the steeply sloping western scarp. Its Post Office building and several farmhouses are of the seventeenth century.*

*Snowshill Lavender Farm*

*Due south of Broadway is Snowshill, one of the highest Cotswold villages, where stone cottages cluster round a sloping green.*

*The centre of the village with the nineteenth-century St. Barnabas Church.*

*Cottages in Stanton.*

These two quiet villages on the Cotswold Way offer many attractive buildings for walkers to enjoy. Both are aptly named; Stanway means stony road and Stanton stony farm.

Stanton's cottages and houses date from the sixteenth and seventeenth centuries when farmers and wool merchants were still prosperous. The village fell into decline as the wool industry collapsed, but was bought in 1906 by the Lancashire architect Sir Philip Stott. He lived at Stanton Court for thirty years during which time he rebuilt and restored many houses.

Stanway is best known for its Elizabethan manor built between 1580 and 1640 by the Tracy family. The manor has changed hands only once in over 1200 years, other than by inheritance, and the houses clustered round it have the architectural unity of an estate village. The remarkably detailed Jacobean gatehouse was thought to have been the work of Inigo Jones but is now attributed to Timothy Strong, the master stonemason from Little Barrington, whose descendants worked on many buildings, including St. Paul's Cathedral.

*Stanton, the main street with the war memorial.*

*Church of St. Peter and cottages in Stanway.*

*Stanway.*

# Temple Guiting and Guiting Power

*Guiting Power.*

South-east of Winchcombe, these two picturesque villages take their names from the 'gushing' waters of the Windrush. They are fine examples of the architectural harmony created by Cotswold masons, the yellow Guiting stone drying out to a golden brown colour.

Temple Guiting is set among trees beside the river Windrush. The village was owned by the Knights Templar in the twelfth century, and it was they who built the earliest recorded fulling mill a little downstream at Barton. St. Mary's Church retains traces of Norman work but has been extensively restored.

Guiting Power lies on a tributary of the Windrush, its russet-coloured houses clustered round a sloping green. The buildings were restored by a self-help housing trust, initially set up for twelve cottages in 1934. The Guiting Manor Amenity Trust is now a self-supporting charity which secures the future of village land. It also ensures that the local community may have access to suitable housing; elsewhere local people are sometimes priced out of the market by incomers.

*Near Guiting Power is the Cotswold Farm Park, with many interesting animal breeds.*

*St. Mary's Church, Temple Guiting.*

*Naunton, a small village south east of the Guitings has pleasant stone buildings including a large old dovecote and a tributary of the Windrush nearby.*

# WINCHCOMBE

Winchcombe could be described as the Cotswolds' first tourist centre, for during medieval times it was second only to Thomas a Becket's tomb as a place of pilgrimage. An abbey was founded here in 768 by King Kenulf of Mercia, dedicated to his martyred young son Kenelm, whose legend brought the pilgrims. The abbey became rich and powerful, building the fine perpendicular church in conjunction with Sir Ralph Boteler of Sudeley.

At the Dissolution of the Monasteries, Lord Seymour of Sudeley destroyed the abbey on Henry VIII's orders. The church of St. Peter remains, noted for the austerity of its style after various restorations. The town's prosperity became dependent on growing tobacco until parliament decreed that the tobacco industry in Virginia should be supported; Samuel Pepys recorded that troops were sent 'to spoil the crop'.

Among the many fine stone buildings are some black and white timbered houses, for Winchcombe is only just within the Cotswolds AONB. Nestling among the hills, surrounded on three sides by high wolds, this attractive town has been popular with many painters.

*The town from the east with Sudeley Castle in the foreground.*

# SUDELEY CASTLE

*The Knot Garden in the Inner Courtyard.*

During the course of its 1000-year history Sudeley has played host to six kings and queens of England. The original eleventh-century castle was rebuilt in the fifteenth century by Ralph Boteler. He was forced to sell the castle to Edward IV who was impressed by its location. In 1547 the castle was given to Sir Thomas Seymour, brother of Jane and husband of Henry VIII's widow Catherine Parr. Her tomb was among the many treasures desecrated during the Civil War.

At the Restoration Sudeley was almost forgotten and its stone was used for building in nearby Winchcombe. In 1837 the Dent family – glovemakers from Worcester – acquired the estate and began restoration, most of which was completed by 1936. Among the remaining ruins is the banqueting hall, suggesting that this was once an imposing royal building.

Visitors to Sudeley can enjoy the nineteenth century gardens as well as St. Mary's church, also built by Ralph Boteler in 1460, and restored by Sir George Gilbert Scott; it has some fine thirteenth-century glass.

*Ruins of the Tithe Barn with the Carp Pond.*

*The Cotswold Scarp at Cleeve Hill.*

*The 'Devil's Chimney' at Leckhampton, with Cheltenham beyond.*

# CHELTENHAM

*Cheltenham College.*

The transformation of the small village of Cheltenham into a Regency Spa began in 1716. William Mason, a local farmer, noticed that flocks of pigeons frequently gathered in a particular field to peck at salt crystals deposited from a spring. He began selling the water in bottles and in 1788 George III gave it his royal approval. Large scale development began after 1816 when the Duke of Wellington was apparently cured of a liver disorder. By the mid-nineteenth century a new town had been created, with classical architecture, wide streets and open spaces, attracting many visitors to take its alkaline waters. While the rural Cotswolds were suffering from depression and poverty, Cheltenham expanded and thrived.

After the Second World War many façades were flaking, but the town has since been revitalized. Its elegant buildings include the Pittville Pump Room, where visitors can still take the waters. The Promenade, now housing municipal offices, is bordered by wide flower beds and a triple avenue of trees, for in this garden town one in every ten acres is public park. There are also two famous public schools.

*The Pittville Pump Room.*

*The Promenade.*

The Abbey and Estate is on the western escarpment of the Cotswolds, some 8 miles from Cheltenham and 4 miles from Gloucester. There is evidence of a link with nearby Gloucester's Benedictine Community from the 12th century, and a manor was established here for the Abbots of Gloucester by 1339. After the Reformation the estate was owned by a series of laymen until it was returned to the Benedictines in 1928, but the community soon outgrew the existing house and a new abbey, clad in Guiting stone, was built.

The former Prinknash Pottery building is now home to the reconstruction of The Great Orpheus Roman pavement from Woodchester.

# GLOUCESTER

*Gloucester Cathedral and the old walls of St Oswald's Priory.*

There has been a settlement here since before the Romans arrived; no evidence of this remains, but there have been major excavations of the Roman city of Glevum. In Saxon times Gloucester became a key garrison city on the Wessex-Mercia border, rivalling London in importance. The Normans built city walls on top of the Roman foundations, and reshaped the Saxon monastery to establish an abbey. The oldest remaining part of the cathedral is the Chapter House, where in 1085 William the Conqueror drew up his plans for the Domesday book.

Beginning in the mid-fourteenth century, the cathedral was slowly re-built, and it was here that master stonemasons broke new architectural ground, pioneering the Perpendicular style that was later adopted in many other cathedrals and churches.

Elizabeth I granted the city a port in 1580, the farthest inland in Britain. It reached its peak in the nineteenth century, playing a key role in the Midlands. The docks have been redeveloped and the Victorian warehouses now accommodate several light industries and museums.

*The National Waterways Museum.*

# Oxfordshire Cotswolds

The eastern Cotswolds slope gently down into Oxfordshire, the rivers flowing towards the Thames. It is along the Windrush that the most typically Cotswold settlements can be found, from the steep hill of popular Burford to the ancient wool town of Witney. The Windrush is the longest Cotswold river, flowing 30 miles from its source near Cutsdean, north-west of Stow, to the Thames at Newbridge. Its clear, swiftly flowing water has a healthy population of trout and attracts many fishermen.

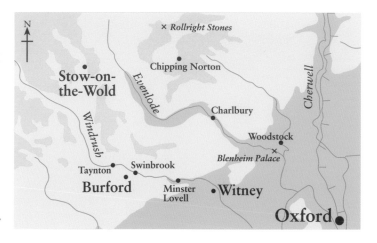

Stretches of the river are still remarkably undisturbed and with sensitive management by riparian owners and the Environment Agency it is hoped that otters will be encouraged to return here. Footprints and spraint have been seen at different locations along the river but there are probably no otters breeding along the Windrush yet.

The highest quality Cotswold stone is found near the Windrush villages north-west of Burford. Known as Taynton stone, it has been famous since the Middle Ages and was even mentioned in the Domesday Book. The two main quarries were in Taynton itself and at Upton in the outskirts of Burford. The stone was used locally but was also transported for use in many well known buildings including St. Paul's Cathedral, St. George's Chapel in Windsor Castle, Blenheim Palace and many of the Oxford colleges. The numerous quarries provided employment for both the labourer and the skilled mason; two families, the Kempsters of Burford and the Strongs of Taynton, produced master masons who worked for Sir Christopher Wren during the seventeenth century.

There are many prehistoric remains in the Cotswolds but the most impressive is probably the Rollright Stones. Situated high on an exposed ridge, this is England's third most important stone circle after Stonehenge and Avebury and is thought to be about 3500 years old. There are many legends and superstitions associated with the stones, which are made even more atmospheric by their bleak and elevated location.

# CHIPPING NORTON

*Almshouses and the church.*

Known locally as 'Chippy', this town on the north-eastern edge of the Cotswolds is at an altitude of 200 meters, catching the worst of winter's storms. The word 'Chipping' comes from cheapen, the medieval term for market; the town prospered as a wool centre, and a busy Wednesday market is still held in the triangular square.

St Mary's Church dates back to the thirteenth century but the nave was rebuilt in 1485 at the expense of a local wool merchant, John Ashfield. The slender pillars and the clerestory windows which form an almost continuous band of glass above the nave give the church great height and lightness, and it is one of the finest interiors among the great Cotswold churches.

Just outside the town stands the Bliss Tweed Mill, designed by George Woodhouse, it looks like a cross between a mansion and a folly rather than a late nineteenth-century factory. Tweed of high quality was made here for many years, but the building has now been converted into flats. The owner William Bliss was instrumental in bringing the railway here, to supply coal for his mill's steam engines.

*Bliss Mill.*

*The Rollright Stones.*

# WOODSTOCK

*Park Street.*

Taynton stone is much in evidence in Woodstock, giving it the feel of a Cotswold town despite the fact that it lies outside the area popularly recognised as 'Cotswold'. The many attractive buildings, as well as Blenheim Palace, attract tourists from far and wide. Few of the buildings are influenced by the exotic Blenheim Palace; most display the simple elegance of the Georgian period. Woodstock has many popular inns, several of which date back to a much older period.

This was an important glove-making town from about 1500 until the last war and visiting monarch were always presented with a pair of gloves.. When gloves were first made here, the nearby Wychwood forest provided plentiful deerskin. The industry grew and during Victorian times there were many small glove factories as well as women hand-stitching at home. Some of the old cottages in the side streets were originally glove-makers' homes.

Today there is an active antique trade carried on by several interesting galleries in the principal streets and a good selection of shops and restaurants.

*Christmas Eve in the centre of the town.*

# BLENHEIM PALACE

*The East Front and Italian Garden.*

There was a royal manor and hunting lodge here from the twelfth century; Henry I made it the first enclosed park in England. It was a favourite residence of Henry II; it is said that he abducted the 15-year-old Fair Rosamund Clifford from Godstow Nunnery, lodging her in a secret bower in Woodstock, near the royal lodge. Edward of Woodstock, known as the Black Prince, was born here in 1330. The royal hunting lodge was destroyed during the Civil War.

In 1705 Queen Anne presented the estate to John Churchill, Duke of Marlborough, in thanks for military victories, in particular the Battle of Blindheim in Bavaria. Woodstock Park became Blenheim and John Vanbrugh was chosen to build a palace in Baroque style, an English version of Versailles, using local stone. Over 1500 craftsmen and labourers were employed to build the seven-acre palace, but progress was slow because the Queen omitted to arrange for timely disbursements of public funds, and it was never entirely clear who was paying. In the 1760s Lancelot Brown was employed to landscape the park; he dammed the river Glyme to form a lake, thereby submerging part of Vanbrugh's bridge.

*The Water Gardens, Upper Terrace fountains.*

*The Lower Terrace and West Front.*

*Dean Jones's room, birthplace of Sir Winston Churchill.*

# MINSTER LOVELL

*The Old Swan.*

Between Burford and Witney, Minster Lovell village and its ruined manor overlook the Windrush. Once a great aristocratic house of Oxfordshire, Minster Lovell Hall was constructed during the fifteenth century by the seventh Lord Lovell. It was built on three sides of a courtyard with the fourth side facing the river; all that remains of the great house are the ruins of the hall, kitchens and dovecote, and its reputed ghosts.

The ninth Lord Lovell, a prominent Yorkist, is said to have hidden here after the defeat of Richard III at Bosworth (1485). No one heard of him again until repairs to the house in 1708 revealed a secret room containing the skeletons of a man and a dog. It is said that the servant who knew of Lovell's presence had died, leaving the master to starve, trapped in his hiding place.

The village has stone and half-timbered cottages, some of which are thatched. The name Minster comes from the church, which once served a small priory. It was rebuilt by William Lovell during the fifteenth century, when the nave was widened, but the tower was rebuilt on its original, narrower, foundations.

*Ruins of the Hall.*

# BURFORD

Burford is often admired for the architectural variety of its steep High Street and smaller side streets. Among the many fourteenth to sixteenth-century stone houses are half-timbered buildings, constructed of oak from Wychwood Forest, once much closer to the town than it is today.

This was an early Windrush crossing where a Saxon settlement clustered round a fort. By 1100 it was a market town, with trading taking place on the flatter part of the wide main street. Along with Northleach it became a leading wool market by 1400, continuing to thrive after the demise of the wool trade as a popular coaching stop. During the eighteenth century, passengers enjoyed Mrs Huntley's delicious biscuits, baked at the local school. Her heirs continued to bake and in 1841 Thomas Huntley went into partnership with the biscuit-tin manufacturer George Palmer in Reading.

The church bears scars from the Civil war when 350 rebellious parliamentarians were imprisoned here by Cromwell; one prisoner scratched his name on the lead font and an exterior wall has bullet marks where three prisoners were shot.

*The Windrush and Church of St. John Baptist.*

*Sheep Street.*

*Stone cottages at the bottom of the High Street.*

*Near the Windrush east of Burford, Swinbrook's stone houses cluster round the Church of St. Mary.*

*The church, inside which six men of the powerful Fettiplace family are remembered by their imposing stone effigies.*

# TAYNTON

This small village of a few old cottages, some farms and a church sits quietly beside the Windrush, belying its former activity. Only the names on the decoratively carved tombstones in the churchyard remind us of the role that Taynton has played in the building of the Cotswolds. Freestone has been quarried here for over 900 years, providing stone of such quality that it was transported to Oxford, to Windsor Castle, and to London from as early as the fourteenth century, and later to St. Paul's Cathedral and to Blenheim Palace. The Taynton entry in Domesday records the quarries and also a wharf on the Thames near Lechlade from where the stone was transported by river. All that remains of most of the quarries are hollows and hummocks on the high ground above the village.

Taynton is one of several small, unspoilt villages along the Windrush near Burford. Little Barrington is built in stone from the hollow round which it stands and is described by Pevsner as 'one of the most appealing village scenes in the Cotswolds'.

*The Village from the south*

# WITNEY

Founded on two traditional sources of Cotswold wealth – wool and swiftly flowing water – Witney produced blankets for over 1000 years. The waters of the Windrush were said to be particularly good for scouring woollen cloth, and Witney blankets were famous for their quality and softness. In 1669 Thomas Early was apprenticed to the wool trade, becoming master-weaver of the town by 1688 when he presented two gold-fringed blankets to James II. Blankets were exported to America from about this time; red and blue blankets were popular with native Americans who exchanged them for furs.

Blanket-making was improved and perfected over the centuries; in 1906 the Early family demonstrated their skill by making a blanket in ten and a half hours, from shearing the sheep to the finished product. In 1969 this record was beaten by more than two hours. The industry closed in the 21st century, there is now a heritage trail marking its history.

Witney is situated on a spur of oolite penetrating well into Oxfordshire. It has many fine stone buildings and has kept the character of a country market town despite quadrupling in population over the past fifty years.

Church Green.

*Church of St. Mary the Virgin.*

Westwell

*The village pond at Westwell, a small village south west of Witney and Burford.*

# Bourton and the Slaughters to the Coln and the Leach

This area includes some of the most visited villages in the Cotswolds, in particular Bourton-on-the-Water and the Slaughters. The combination of pretty Cotswold stone cottages alongside the clear water of the river Windrush and their proximity to the Fosse Way has helped to make them popular.

Built as a military road by the Romans, the Fosse once went from Exeter to Lincoln and is still a major route through the Cotswolds. For much of its length the road pays little heed to contours, going straight up over the hills and down into valleys like a switchback. The Fosse was routed with remarkable accuracy; the middle 150 miles never depart from the direct line by more than 6.5 miles. Where a bend was necessary it was usually on a hill top, from where the sightings were taken. In some places the road was built up above the surrounding land on an agger, making it easier to defend. It is thought that the Fosse was built as the spine of a defence system between Lincoln and Cirencester, connecting important military bases and providing better protection over a wide area by allowing for rapid deployment of troops. Many medieval and more

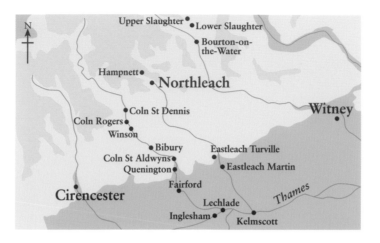

recent villages lie within two miles of the Fosse but very few are situated on it.

The sources of many well-known Cotswold streams are found on these high wolds; the Coln, the Leach and the Windrush all flow down winding, picturesque valleys to become rivers as they cross the Oxford Vale to join the Thames. They have escaped recent industrialization, but the many old mills bear witness to a time when water was an important source of power.

Perhaps the best way to explore the Cotswolds is on foot along one of the many well-maintained and clearly signed footpaths. There are several long-distance routes, the best known of which is probably the Cotswold Way, covering 100 miles on its journey from Chipping Campden to Bath. In 1996 the Macmillan Way was opened, a 235-mile walk following the oolitic limestone belt from Rutland to Dorset. Established to increase awareness of the Cancer Relief Macmillan Fund, the route crosses the heart of the Cotswolds giving the walker a real insight into the character of the area.

# BOURTON-ON-THE-WATER

During the Iron Age a large fort was built at Salmonsbury, to the east of Bourton; later the Romans built a bridge to carry the Fosse Way. At that time it was the natural capital of the northern Cotswolds, being at a junction of two Roman roads and three rivers. The Saxons probably had a minor capital here; in 1931 the site of an Anglo-Saxon hut was excavated, revealing the remains of an upright loom. This is some of the earliest evidence of the wool-processing industry.

Straddling the Windrush, this village has been described as 'unashamedly pretty' with its series of low stone bridges beside neat tree-shaded greens and tidy stone banks. Standing back from the river are traditional Cotswold buildings, many of which are now tourist shops for the day-trippers and visitors. There has been a church here since Saxon times, but the unusual domed church we see today is of the nineteenth century, to a design by Sir Thomas G. Jackson in which he retained the fourteenth-century chancel and the Georgian tower. The result is an outstanding building of which the architect was justly proud.

*The Model Village.*

*Summer.*

*Autumn.*

*Winter.*

*Lower Slaughter.*

These villages beside the little Eye stream owe their unusual name to the wet land or 'slough' upon which they lie, and they are famous for their unspoilt stone buildings in traditional Cotswold style. Local quarries supplied the stone and slate, the quality of which made it worth transporting to Oxford as early as 1452 to roof New College.

The stream flowing through Lower Slaughter is crossed by a series of small bridges and bordered by quaint cottages. It is forded beside an old watermill with a brick tower, built in the early nineteenth century. The manor house, now a hotel, was built by the Cotswold master mason Valentine Strong about 1650.

In 1906 eight cottages in the central square of Upper Slaughter were restored and remodelled by Sir Edwin Lutyens. The Manor House, once entered under a record of sale from the eighteenth century as the 'Slaughter House', typifies the local style of architecture and was described by Herbert Evans in 1905 as 'one of the most beautiful in the Cotswolds'.

The church of St. Peter in Upper Slaughter retains some Norman features after careful restoration in 1877.

*The Eye at Lower Slaughter.*

*Upper Slaughter.*

*At Upper Slaughter.*

# NORTHLEACH

The modest size of this small town belies its former importance as a Cotswold wool centre. The Abbey of Gloucester owned the area from AD800, granting the town a charter in 1220 to hold a weekly market. This small market town was transformed by the wool trade, and in 1340-1540 it flourished as the centre of a large sheep-rearing area.

Northleach has long been linked with transport; the Fosse Way lies just to the west and about AD300 the Salt Way trade route came through the town, used for carrying salt by packhorse from salt mines at Droitwich to the Thames at Lechlade. During the age of coach travel it was a centre for changing horses and refreshing passengers on the London-Gloucester route. Northleach has good pubs and restaurants, an excellent wine merchant, a butcher, a baker, a Post Office and a general stores as well as the Keith Harding World of Mechanical Music.

West of the town lies the eighteenth-century 'house of correction', the design of which was copied in prisons in America, it has been used as a police station, museum, as well as offices and now partly houses The Cotswolds Conservation Board.

*The fifteenth-century Church of St. Peter and St. Paul.*

*On a hill north-west of Northleach is the tiny village of Hampnett. Evidence of its long history includes a long barrow and remains of a deserted medieval settlement.*

*The interior of the largely Norman church was gaudily painted in 1871 by a Victorian vicar trying to recreate the style of a medieval building.*

# THE COLN VILLAGES

*Vicarage and Church at Coln St. Aldwyns.*

This gentle valley with its woods and water-meadows contains several quiet villages, with old watermills, large stone barns and small churches dating from the Saxons and Normans. The river Coln meanders through the Cotswolds for the whole of its 25 miles, with trout thriving in its clear waters. Coln St. Aldwyns has seventeenth-century cottages clustered round a green, and nineteenth-century estate cottages in the same style. The earliest masonry in the church of St. John the Baptist is Norman but it has been much altered. John Keble was vicar here from 1782 to 1835 but lived in nearby Fairford, where his father was parish priest. Coln Rogers, named after its 11th century patron Roger de Gloucester, lies in a broad valley. Hidden amongst trees along a quiet walled lane is the church of St. Andrew with its Saxon nave and chancel remaining almost intact. The northernmost Coln village is Coln St. Dennis with its Norman church and some fine seventeenth-century stone barns. The twelfth-century church of St. Swithin at Quenington was heavily restored in 1882 but fortunately retains two exceptionally fine Norman doorways and tympana.

*Coln St. Aldwyns.*

*Coln Rogers.*

*Coln St. Dennis.*

*South of Coln St. Aldwyns is Quenington, the name means 'Farmstead of Women'.*

*Twelfth-century carved doorway, St. Swithin's church at Quenington.*

# BIBURY

Situated on the River Coln, Bibury has been popular with visitors since it was 'discovered' by William Morris at the turn of the century. He described it as the 'most beautiful village in England', and except for the visitors and their cars it has probably changed very little. The village centre clusters round a square near St. Mary's, a Saxon church. Some of the Saxon remains inside the church are casts as the originals are housed in the British Museum.

Overlooking a water-meadow and the river is Arlington Row, a group of cottages with steeply pitched stone roofs. The original medieval house and store was converted in the seventeenth century into 'one-up-one-down' weavers' cottages. These individually plain cottages are made picturesque by their grouping and situation. Their inhabitants would have worked hard for a low wage, providing cloth for fulling at Arlington Mill. There has probably been a mill here since Domesday, but the mill we see today is seventeenth-century and has been used for both cloth and corn; it has now been converted into a tourist attraction.

*Arlington Row.*

*The Trout Farm (1902), covers 15 acres, 5 are open for fishing, picnicking or feeding the fish. On average 500,000 fish are produced for sale per year.*

*River Coln in spring.*

*The early Norman Church of St. Michael's in Winson consists of nave and chancel only. The sloping churchyard has fine eighteenth-century table tombs.*

*The Village has a pretty collection of cottages and an imposing manor house.*

# FAIRFORD

This town on the river Coln has great spaciousness because of its open water-meadows. There was an Anglo-Saxon community and river crossing here; now it is a fine old market town with an interesting 'wool' church.

The wealthy wool merchant John Tame was responsible for rebuilding Fairford church between 1491 and 1497, and his son continued the work after his death in 1500. The church is renowned for its 28 stained glass windows, the only complete set of medieval windows to survive in a British parish church. They are largely undamaged, having survived wars and vandalism since their installation began in 1500. Some of the biblical figures in the windows may be hidden portraits of Henry VII and his family.

A memorial in the church records the death in 1866 of John Keble, born in 1792 at Fairford where his father was Rector. A prolific poet, Fellow of Oriel College, and a founder of the Oxford Movement, Keble is remembered by the Oxford college that bears his name. After graduating brilliantly John Keble left Oxford to be his father's curate at Fairford, where he worked in the parish like any other curate.

*On the Coln, leading from the water-meadows.*

Although Lechlade is on the Thames it is a Cotswold town with many stone houses and a fine fifteenth-century 'wool' church built of Taynton stone. Nevertheless it also has much in common with Thames valley towns and has long been an important transport link. For centuries Lechlade was on one of the main trade arteries west from London, by both road and river. This is still the highest point of navigation on the Thames and here the Thames and Severn Canal once branched off to Stroud. Leisure boats have replaced the trading vessels for Lechlade is now a favourite mooring place.

Near the confluence of the Thames and the Leach is St. John's bridge, reputed to be the first stone bridge over the Thames outside London. The original structure dates from 1229, but it was rebuilt about 1830. This was one of the places where stone from the quarries at Taynton was put onto barges for transport downstream, where it was used in many buildings including Windsor Castle, many Oxford colleges and St. Paul's Cathedral. Near the bridge is St. John's lock overlooked by a statue purporting to be Father Thames, brought here from its original site near the source of the river.

*Lechlade*

*St. John's Lock and the Thames.*

*The Church of St. Lawrence at the end of the school day.*

*The quiet riverside village of Kelmscott, near Lechlade, was where William Morris had his country home in the Elizabethan manor house from 1871 until 1896.*

*This hamlet on the Thames is noted for the Church of St. John the Baptist, a thirteenth-century building saved by William Morris from Victorian restoration.*

# THE EASTLEACH VILLAGES

An old clapper footbridge over the Leach separates the two peaceful villages of Eastleach Martin, known locally as Bouthrop, and Eastleach Turville. The bridge is named after Keble, for a family of that name held the manor of Eastleach Turville for five generations during the fifteenth century. The better known John Keble was non-resident curate of both churches for eight years after his ordination in 1815.

It was because each village was owned by a different Lord that the two churches were built so close together. St. Andrew's Church in Eastleach Turville has an early fourteenth-century saddleback tower. Within view of St. Andrew's, Bouthrop's Church of St. Michael and St. Martin is now in the care of the Redundant Churches Fund. This humble church has remained remarkably unspoilt, with old oil lamps, seventeenth century pews and even some late medieval benches.

Eastleach Turville has several estate cottages on the hill, and a large house with a nineteenth-century gothic wing overlooking the verdant valley where the river is bordered by reeds, willowherb and irises.

*The Church of St. Michael and St. Martin at Eastleach Martin or Bouthrop.*

# CIRENCESTER AND STROUD AREA

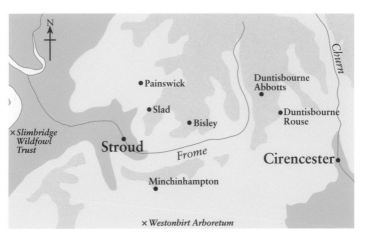

The western Cotswolds has a feeling very different from the rest of the area, in terms of landscape, vegetation and settlement. The differences can be largely accounted for by geology; on the escarpment there are steep slopes and behind it valleys tumble down to meet at Stroud. This is the most densely wooded part of the Cotswolds, with beech-dominated 'hanging' woodlands covering some of the higher ground above the steep, grassy valleys. In other areas, such as around Minchinhampton, vast swathes of rolling common-land occupy the higher ground. The fast-flowing streams lent themselves well to wool-processing. Industrialization started in the 1750s; numerous mills were built and the development of canals and railways helped to turn the hamlet of Stroud into a prosperous town at the heart of one of the principal manufacturing areas of the country. Massingham said of the Stroudwater Hills that 'Industry and beauty once lived together in peace'; this may have been true for some, but for many of the cottage-based weavers it was probably a pretty harsh existence. The industry brought many people, and the area round Stroud remains more densely populated than the rest of the Cotswolds.

There was a great deal of early settlement in the area; the strategically important escarpment is dotted with the remains of Iron Age forts such as that at Painswick Beacon where the earthworks are still very much in evidence. About 250 acres of this area are common land, popular with walkers and offering views over Gloucester towards Wales to the west, and eastwards over the Painswick valley.

The road from Stroud to Cirencester initially follows the Chalford valley and the river Frome, beside which there are over 30 mills. The road then climbs out of the valley and soon enters more familiar Cotswold land, running beside a long stone wall surrounding Lord Bathurst's 10,000-acre Cirencester Park. Cirencester, the largest of the region's towns, has claimed to be the Capital of the Cotswolds, standing at the meeting of three important Roman roads.

'Painswick sprawls white in the other valley, like the skeleton of a foundered mammoth'. Laurie Lee's vivid description aptly recalls the colour of the pale grey stone and the buildings climbing up the hillside. There are many fine houses here, reflecting the town's former prosperity during three hundred years of activity in the cloth industry.

St. Mary's Church is largely of the fifteenth and sixteenth centuries but the spire was not added until 1632. The spire was struck by lightning in 1793, and again in 1883. The church was occupied by Parliamentarians during the Civil War; scars of bullets and cannon shots remain on the tower walls. The churchyard is famed for its 99 clipped yew trees and the collection of table tombs intricately carved by local masons. Most of the yews were planted about 1792 and it is said that every time a hundredth tree is planted it dies. In recent years the yew clippings have been used by a French company to manufacture a drug that helps cancer patients.

Painswick contains many notable houses built in the prosperous seventeenth century, many of them in the outskirts of this fair-sized town.

*The town from the east.*

*The Rococo Garden at Painswick, known for striking floral displays, including snowdrops in early spring.*

# STROUD

*Converted mill.*

When Daniel Defoe visited Stroud on his travels through Britain in the early eighteenth century, he saw crimson and scarlet broadcloth being made for the king. Stroudwater scarlets and Uley blues were famous throughout Europe and were in great demand for military uniforms.

Located at the convergence of five deep river valleys, Stroud made a natural industrial centre for the Cotswolds. By the time of Defoe's visit there were 150 fulling mills in the Chalford valley, otherwise known as the Golden Valley because of the wealth it generated for cloth merchants. The town was built upon the wool industry and suffered greatly when many cloth mills closed during the nineteenth century. Several mills are still working but only one produces cloth; Lodgemore Mill dyes cloth and finishes it for use in billiard and snooker tables as well as covering for tennis balls.

Stroud hosts an increasing number of festivals, including an Art Festival 'The Stroud Fringe' in the second week of May and since the 1950s the 'Stroud International Brick and Rolling Pin Throwing Contest' in July. This unusual event attracts teams from many countries.

*One of the valleys leading to the town.*

# SLAD

Slad takes its name from the little Slade stream running through the valley south of Painswick to join the Frome at Stroud. Much of the village is beside a busy road down to Stroud, but a little lane takes the visitor down into the valley and the Slad written about by Laurie Lee. Stone houses cling to the hillsides and up above are the beech woods which defined the ' limits of his world'.

Like the other western valleys, there are green pastures below and woodland on the higher slopes and hilltops. Most of the grassland is very different from the flower-rich meadows of Laurie Lee's childhood, but on the other side of the valley from Slad is the Gloucestershire Wildlife Trust's Elliott Nature Reserve. This hillside appears brown in comparison with the lush green of the surrounding grassland, but in summer closer inspection reveals orchids among the rich sward of wild flowers and clouds of butterflies. This unimproved grassland, untouched by fertilizers and herbicides, is grazed by cattle in accordance with conservation plans. The Church of the Holy Trinity was built in the 1830s by Charles Baker of Painswick.

# BISLEY

*Cottages leading to the church.*

An old Western Cotswold rhyme describes some of its settlements thus;

Mincing Hampton and Painswick Proud

Beggarly Bisley and Strutting Stroud

The source of this may have been a government report on the local wool industry in the 1820s, which found that 2000 of Bisley's 6000 people were unemployed; indeed the village was not alone in suffering with the wool industry's decline. In earlier times, wealthy clothiers had built fine houses here, and nowadays this unspoilt village clinging to the hillside has a more prosperous air and harbours many antique shops.

Bisley is probably best known for its Well-Dressing Ceremony on Ascension Day, when its seven springs are decorated with garlands of flowers. Known as the Bisley Wells, the gabled water chutes were restored for Thomas Keble in 1863. Brother of the more famous John, he was vicar of All Saints Church where a thirteenth-century 'poor souls' light is found in the churchyard. This small hexagonal building where candles were lit and masses were said for the poor is thought to be the only example in England.

# THE DUNTISBOURNE VALLEY

*Duntisbourne Rouse.*

To the west of Ermin Street lies a steep, secluded valley along Dunt's bourne or stream. It is easily accessible from Cirencester yet has remained quietly rural and unspoilt. Duntisbourne Rouse is barely a village; a few farm cottages cluster near a ford and the tiny Church of St. Michael which has Saxon origins. One of the smallest Cotswold churches, it was not noticed by the wealthy wool merchants and has retained its Saxon nave and west wall as well as its largely early Norman chancel.

Further up the valley Duntisbourne Leer, once in the possession of the Abbey of Lire in Normandy, has stone buildings attractively grouped round a clear ford. Several of the houses have pigeon lofts in their gable ends, and the cottages, farmhouses and barns all have similar proportions. Water Lane links this village to Duntisbourne Abbots; closed to vehicles, this lane follows the course of the stream and was apparently used for washing cartwheels. Abbots, the largest of the villages, descends in terraces down the steep valley sides. A hamlet, Middle Duntisbourne, completes this ancient group.

*Duntisbourne Leer.*

# CIRENCESTER

The Roman settlement of Corinium was the second largest town in Britain. It was initially a military base, strategically situated at the junction of the Fosse Way, Akeman Street and Ermin street. Later it was laid out as a town, becoming the administrative centre for the Dobunni, the native British tribe living in the southern Cotswolds. The Saxons destroyed it in 577 but the town regained some of its status under Norman rule, and later became a prosperous medieval wool town.

Cirencester's market square is dominated by the cathedral-like St. John Baptist Church. The large south porch with its impressive fan vaulting was built about 1490, providing an office for the Abbey's secular wool business. Following the Dissolution it became the Town Hall and was not returned to the church until 1671. The massive tower was begun soon after 1400, built with King Henry IV's reward after townspeople had seized three rebellious earls and effectively prevented civil war. The town contains many interesting buildings spanning several centuries, and a now grass-grown Roman amphitheatre.

Minchinhampton is surrounded by common land high above the Chalford valley. A long narrow street bordered by stone cottages leads to a compact centre clustered round a pillared market-house built in the seventeenth century and given to the town in 1919 by the Lord of the Manor.

Holy Trinity church is cruciform and has a distinctive truncated spire; part of the spire was demolished in 1563 because it was too heavy for the supporting arches. Although there has been a church here since Norman times, the oldest remaining parts of the present church are the fourteenth-century transepts and tower; the south transept is especially fine.

The National Trust bought Minchinhampton Common before the Second World War in order to control quarrying. Together with Rodborough Common it covers nearly 1,000 acres of high open grassland and woods, and is bordered by small groups of old weavers' houses and other more modern but pleasant enough buildings. The common is pockmarked with a variety of earthworks from Neolithic barrows and old quarries to modern golf bunkers.

*The Town Clock Tower.*

*A pleasant market town on the western edge of the Cotswolds south of Stroud.*

# SLIMBRIDGE

Slimbridge has been a landmark for UK wildlife conservation for over 50 years. Artist and naturalist Sir Peter Scott recognised the importance of the fertile fields beside the Severn as rich winter feeding grounds for huge flocks of migratory ducks, geese and swans. He believed in bringing wildlife and people together for the benefit of both, creating an internationally important 800 acre nature reserve where visitors can view thousands of wild birds. Slimbridge successfully combines providing a high profile visitor attraction while playing a key role in the conservation of wetland wildlife through habitat management and a wide reaching education programme. It also has the world's largest collection of exotic wildfowl, helping many endangered species through captive breeding.

Today Slimbridge is the headquarters of the Wildfowl and Wetlands Trust, the only charity devoted to the conservation of wetlands and their wildlife. There are seven other WWT reserves around the country and The Wetland Centre opened in London in 2000.

*Uley is a small village 6 miles south west of Stroud. As well as interesting buildings it is home to the Uley Brewery, known for the quality of its fine beer.*

*A Tudor Manor house (1450–1616) near Uley, standing in its own formal garden and surrounded by medieval landmark buildings.*

*Wotton sits under the Southern edge of the Cotswolds. The Cotswold Way passes along the main shopping streets in the centre, which is a Conservation Area.*

# WESTONBIRT ARBORETUM

Founded in 1829 by landowner Robert Holford, Westonbirt Arboretum possesses over 18,000 numbered tree specimens within 600 acres. Visitors are rewarded by flowering cherries, rhododendrons and azaleas in spring, shady glades and sunny rides in summer, shapes of conifers contrasted with coloured stems of birches and dogwoods in winter. But most famous are the autumn colours, produced mainly by Japanese maples, American oaks and hickories, Chinese cherries and the Katsura tree.

Robert Holford and his son George funded plant hunting expeditions, grew and propagated unusual plants and by careful planting created dramatic contrasts of colour and texture. Their vision has produced one of the world's best tree collections, including many species now rare in the wild. In Silkwood, an area of ancient native woodlands, a small leaved lime has been aged at 2000 years.

The Forestry Commission have managed Westonbirt since 1956. Propagation is a vital management tool, both to ensure the arboretum's future and to maintain the quality of this internationally important gene bank.

# TETBURY

*The Market House.*

Tetbury's hub is the Market House, from which the town's streets radiate. Built in 1655, probably for weighing wool, it is supported by 22 stone pillars and continues to be used for markets and meetings. Situated only 2 miles from the Fosse Way, Tetbury has been a busy market town since it received a charter in the thirteenth century. Like so many other Cotswold towns, it prospered with the wool trade and went through a building boom in the sixteenth and seventeenth centuries.

The tall, elegant spire of St. Mary's Church is claimed to be among the highest in the United Kingdom. Although the spire and tower are only about one hundred years old, they were built as close copies of the medieval original. The rest of the church dates from the eighteenth century; its airy interior owes much to the very large windows, which contain pieces of medieval glass.

Tetbury has a prosperous air, due in part to the proximity of Highgrove and Gatcombe. Several shops and businesses display the emblem of three feathers, indicating they are 'By Appointment to HRH the Prince of Wales'.

*St. Mary's Church and outskirts of the town.*

# BATH

Bath is best known for its classical architecture and its development as a Roman city 'Aquae Sulis'. The presence of hot springs and easily worked stone made it attractive to the Romans who built an impressive town, which flourished for nearly 400 years. It declined rapidly after the Romans left Britain and did not thrive again until the eighteenth century, when once again it was water and stone that made it great.

The entrepreneur Ralph Allen first realized the potential of the local stone for classical building. Having made his fortune reorganizing the country's postal service, he bought Combe Down quarries and provided the raw material for the architects John Wood elder and younger. Under the inspiration of Beau Nash an elegant and fashionable city grew up, attracting visitors to take its waters and enjoy the social life.

A dream of angels climbing ladders to heaven instructed Oliver King, Bishop of Bath and Wells in the early sixteenth century, to replace the Norman cathedral with a new building. The Abbey's west front was dictated by the dream and there is much fine stonework in the building.

*The city centre.*

*The River Avon and Pulteney Bridge*

*The Royal Crescent.*

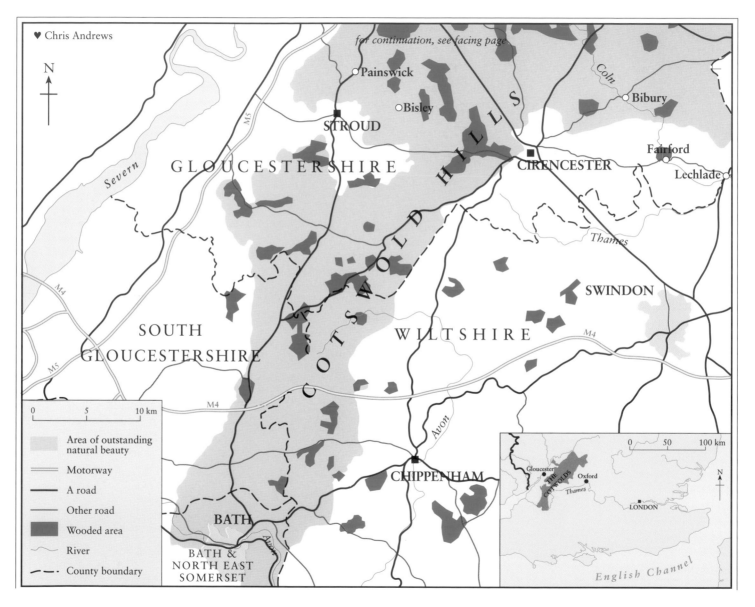

♥ Chris Andrews

N

*for continuation, see facing page*

○Painswick

Coln

○Bisley

○Bibury

■ STROUD

GLOUCESTERSHIRE

COTSWOLD  HILLS

■ CIRENCESTER

Fairford

Lechlade○

Severn

M5

Thames

SWINDON

SOUTH
GLOUCESTERSHIRE

COTSWOLD

WILTSHIRE

M4

M4

M5

Avon

0      5      10 km

Area of outstanding
natural beauty

Motorway

A road

Other road

Wooded area

River

County boundary

CHIPPENHAM

BATH

Avon

BATH &
NORTH EAST
SOMERSET

0      50      100 km

Gloucester
THE
COTSWOLDS
Oxford
Thames

LONDON

N

English Channel

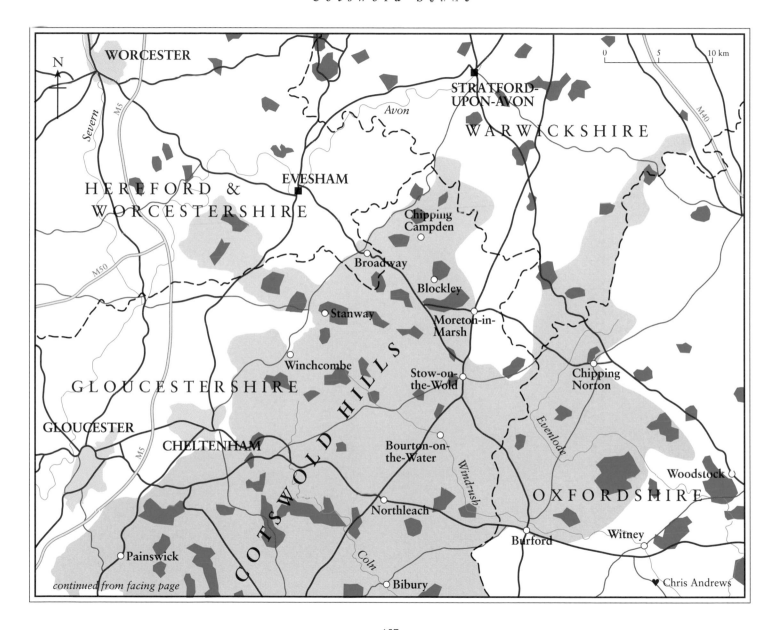

# Index